Old COATBRIDGE

by

Campbell McCutcheon

On the Canal, Coatbridge

LANARKSHIRE HERITAGE SERIES

First Published in the United Kingdom, 1993
Reprinted 1995
By Richard Stenlake, Ochiltree Sawmill, The Lade,
Ochiltree, Ayrshire KA18 2NX
Tel: 01290 700266

ISBN 1-872074-29-4

INTRODUCTION

Little is known of the early inhabitants of the Monklands but the area has been inhabited for the last five or six thousand years. The earliest settlement discovered was at Woodend Loch, where some early Stone Age tools were found in the peat bog. Other late settlements have been found at Annathill and at Drumpellier, including an Iron Age crannog (artificial island) on Lochend Loch. This would have been inhabited from 100BC until after the Romans had left Scotland for good. There is no evidence of Roman occupation even though they controlled this part of Scotland for a time.

In 1162, King Malcolm IV granted the lands which were later to be called the Monklands to the Cistercian Monks of Newbattle Abbey. This is the first written record of the area. The monks farmed and cultivated the district. A sheep grange was established at Drumpellier and the wool transported along the King's Highway to the east. Around 1220 a corn mill was constructed on the North Calder Water at Haggs. Coal was also hewn from outcrops by the monks, who had experience of mining from owning the lead mines at Wanlockhead. Little of importance happened in the area until the 1700s. The land that was to become Coatbridge was dissected by the main road from Edinburgh to Glasgow and there was relatively easy access to the nearby markets of Glasgow for the produce of the area.

By the 1790s most of the agricultural land had been improved and there was much natural as well as managed woodland. The rivers were well stocked with salmon and trout and the land extremely fertile. Coal was being mined on a small scale and the Monkland Canal had been built to transport this coal to the ready market of Glasgow. The roads in the area had been improved and there was a toll on the Glasgow-Airdrie Turnpike at Langloan. Old Monkland had thirty public houses to serve the population of about 4000.

One of the main occupations was weaving and over 400 people (mainly men) were employed in what was one of the better paid industries of the period. Over 200 girls, some as young as eight, were also employed in ancillary trades. A brick and tile works was built in 1785 on the banks of the Monkland Canal. Here were manufactured pan and slate tiles. In 1788 the works were extended and a pottery added, built here because of the abundance of cheap coal in the neighbourhood. The few coal mines employed just over 400 colliers but more were being opened all the time.

David Mushet's discovery, in 1805, of blackband ironstone, a rock containing iron nodules in a bed of coal like rock, helped to seal the future of Coatbridge as Scotland's Iron Burgh. This rich ore was first discovered at Coatdyke but it wasn't until twenty or so years had passed that the benefits of the blackband ironstone were felt. The technology of the time could not cope with the coal rich ironstone. The breakthrough came in 1828 when J.B. Neilson discovered and patented the hot blast process. Hot air was introduced to the furnace and this more than halved its coal consumption. The Bairds of Gartsherrie, farmers to trade, already leased two coal mines from the Colts and saw the new process as a way of utilising some of their production. In May 1830 their new blast furnace was lit for the first time. A new era had dawned for the Coatbridge area.

Expansion was rapid and others followed quickly having seen the money-making potential of the new process. All along the canal banks there were new furnaces and malleable ironworks attracted by the ready supply of ore and coal, cheap transport of the raw materials and cooling water for the furnaces. Railways were also being built at a prodigious rate to transport raw materials from further afield, to remove slag and waste to the many bings which were beginning to tower over the landscape and to take the finished iron away to the ports in Glasgow for export worldwide. The smoke, heat, light and noise went on 24 hours a day, seven days a week. "Hell with the lid off" was how one correspondent described the town.

The population expanded rapidly as the new furnaces and mines were opened and required labour. In 1821 the population was just under 7000, but by 1841 had grown to 19707. Only ten years later it had gone up to 27332. Houses were thrown up to accommodate the influx of people and this led to the creation of slums in and around the town. Coatbridge did not gain Burgh status until 1885. When it did, it had to conform to some of the Public Health Acts regarding pollution and overcrowding. The Burgh was formed by the amalgamation of the settlements of Coatbridge, Gartsherrie, Whifflet, Langloan, Dundyvan, Old Monkland and Dunbeth. By this time the beginning of the end was in sight for the iron industry in Coatbridge. Local reserves of ironstone were almost worked out and steel was beginning to take over as the dominant metal used by industry. The First World War helped to keep the failing industry alive for a few more years, but the 1920s saw the death knell for many of the local foundries and furnaces.

There were other changes taking place in the town at that time also. The atrocious housing had been condemned and new houses "fit for heroes" were being constructed. Cliftonville, at Coatdyke, replaced some of the rows of slums that had predominated there. The town also lost the Rosehall Rows, which were amongst the worst housing in the United Kingdom. The Depression hit Coatbridge badly and, when Stewart & Lloyds opened their new integrated steelworks at Corby in 1934, many of the younger inhabitants moved away in the hope of starting a better life in Northamptonshire. Only Gartsherrie survived the 1930s and it closed in 1967, finally ending an era that had lasted for only about 150 years.

Since World War Two, the town has expanded outwards, towards the A8, which has been the focus for most of the new industry to come to the area. All of the old slums have gone, replaced by housing schemes at Old Monkland, Kirkwood, Kirkshaws and Carnbroe. Light industries have replaced heavy industry, although specialised metalworking and engineering still flourish in Coatbridge. The eighties have seen attempts to develop the Monklands in general, and Coatbridge in particular, as a centre for tourism. The site of Summerlee ironworks is now an established industrial museum and the town has the Time Capsule, as well as Drumpellier Country Park and the new Quadrant shopping centre. Much of the wasteland left as the only reminder of once great industrial concerns has been landscaped or built on. The bings have become the foundations for new roads and little now remains as evidence of Coatbridge's past as Scotland's Iron Burgh.

Old Monkland Parish Church in 1904. The church was built in 1790 although there had been an ecclesiastical site here for centuries beforehand. Sometime about 1850 an unusual phenomenon was discovered. After opening the grave of James Merry, who had died around 1807-8, to bury one of his relatives, it was discovered that his body was whole and had petrified into a hard blue substance. The body had a chalk-like appearance and crumbled after a few hours exposure. It was guessed that minerals in the water had caused this transformation. After this discovery a few other petrified bodies were found in the churchyard.

Old Monkland Public School

The pupils pose for a postcard publisher sometime about 1908. Old Monkland Public School was the original Parish school for the area and is long gone, having been demolished years ago. In the 1790s there were five schools in the whole Parish.

Built in the early 1840s, the Rosehall rows were some of the worst houses in the whole of Scotland. The Royal Commission on Housing in Scotland reported in 1914 that "in some of the rows seven or eight people occupy a single room". Rain water ran down the walls and the outside closets were "in a state of revolting filth". The man responsible for them was Robert Addie who owned Langloan Iron Works as well as the Rosehall pits. This view is of Front Row leading onto Whifflet Street. These slums were demolished in the 1920s but were made infamous in George Orwell's 'Road to Wigan Pier'. A photograph of the rows appeared on the cover of this book about housing conditions for the working classes in England (!)

A 1970s high rise block of flats and a concrete shopping centre have replaced the buildings on the right. The smoke screen is coming from amongst others, Lochrin Iron Works, Calder Iron Works, the Tinplate Works and Tennant's Foundry. Little now remains to suggest that this area was once a major industrial centre. The land beyond the railway has lain derelict for years and is only now being rejuvenated and landscaped. Only Tennants remains as one of Coatbridge's last bastions of heavy industry.

Timothy Pont's map (published 1654) mentions this area as being called Wheatflat, probably a reference to the use of the land by the monks. It is hard to imagine Whifflet as lush green fields today. Two hundred years of industrial use have taken their toll and much of Whifflet is still derelict. The west side of Whifflet Street has survived rather well but the other side has had its character totally destroyed by 'improvements'. As one of the main roads to the M8, Whifflet Street is permanently chock-a-block with traffic.

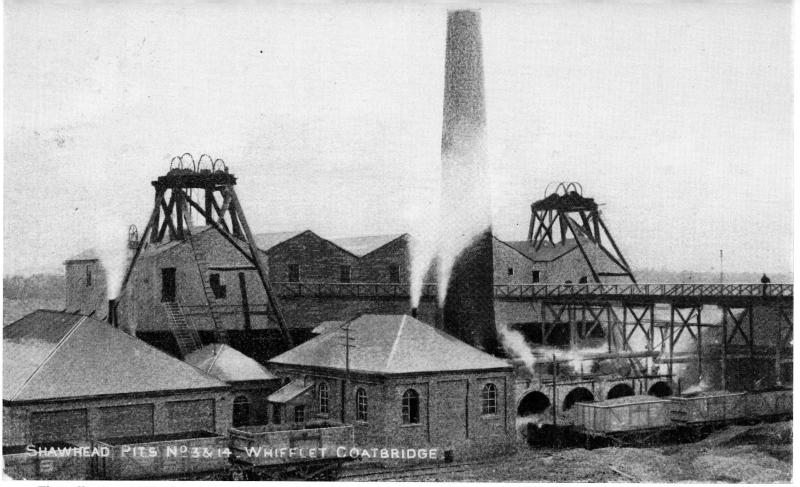

SHAWHEAD PITS Nº 3 & 14 WHIFFLET COATBRIDGE

The collieries at Whifflet produced both coal and ironstone. It was the location of the raw materials close at hand that contributed to the phenomenal growth of Coatbridge. By the early 1860s it was recognised that the reserves of local ironstone and coal were running out and the raw material to power the blast furnaces was already being imported from elsewhere in Scotland, notably from Denny, Kilsyth, Bathgate and Wilsontown, as well as from Ireland and Spain. There were about seventy collieries in operation then. Only seventy years earlier there had been four. Decline was slow as some of the smaller seams were mined but most of the collieries did not last to the beginning of this century. By the end of the Second World War mining was becoming a distant memory to most.

Whifflet Salvation Army Band circa 1919 with Bandmaster John Carson.

Drumpellier House was originally built in 1741 and was owned by the Buchanan family. The Buchanans made a fortune from the Virginia Tobacco trade and used the money to beautify and improve the lands of Drumpellier. The canal was built through part of the estate and the Buchanans also bought part of the estate of Dundyvan for £3500. Part of the land was sold for the Dundyvan furnaces at a cost of £14000 and what remained in 1844 was still worth over £20000. The lands of Drumpellier were donated to the Burgh in 1919. Sadly, the house was demolished in the late 1960s to make way for the golf club car park.

Janet Hamilton, whose house is seen above, was a local poetess born near Shotts in 1795. By the age of five, she had taught herself to read. In 1809 she married John Hamilton, her father's employee in his shoe makers. When she was in her fifties she taught herself to write and wrote some pieces for a magazine called 'Working Man's Friend'. Later a collection of her poems were published in book form. Her work was simple but admired for its integrity and honesty.

Looking back towards the Cross, this 1904 view shows Bank Street in all its former glory. Along the bank of the canal, the warehouses and timber yard have gone. The canal itself was infilled in the 1960s and has been piped underground. On the right, nothing remains of this once substantial street. The Time Capsule, Coatbridge's new leisure pool, sits like some futuristic Star Trek set on the remains of Bank Street's tenements.

BANK STREET, COATBRIDGE.

Looking the other way, towards Langloan, the Time Capsule starts on the left. When this view was taken around 1910, the cinema was a relatively new thing. Thousands would flock daily, after work, to see the latest movie and every town could boast at least two or three cinemas. Coatbridge was no exception and had the Empire and Regal amongst others.

Bain's moved their factory lock, stock and barrel from the Lochrin area of Edinburgh and built a new factory at Whifflet. This was to take advantage of the easy access by rail and ability to expand. The works opened at the beginning of this century and were located next to Sheepford Goods Station and the tinplate works. This view shows one of their lorries sometime in the 1920s. Part of the works still survive at Summerlee having been moved to the Museum in the mid 1980s.

Baird St Coatbridge.

It was the Bairds of Gartsherrie who were ultimately responsible for the street layout in central Coatbridge. Originally farmers, they expanded into coal mining and from there into iron. There were seven brothers in total and they opened their first blast furnace in 1830 at Gartsherrie using the newly developed blast process. Originally, cold air had been introduced to the furnace to smelt the iron but in 1828, J.B. Neilson of the Glasgow Iron Works (a friend of the Bairds), discovered that if hot air was introduced to the furnace much less coal was used to produce iron. It was this process that was to make the Bairds' second and largest fortune. They began to purchase land and mineral rights all around the district as a means of keeping their furnaces fed with the raw materials required. The land for Dunbeth Hill was bought between 1834 and 1851 and the Bairds began to plan the development of this area.

One of the first buildings to be built was the ubiquitous church. Gartsherrie Church was built using donations mainly from the Baird brothers but also from the Colts who had sold the land in 1837. It was completed in 1839 and became the first church in Coatbridge. As feu superiors, the Bairds could stipulate the types and quality of houses to be built on their land and so this area has some larger houses with ashlar frontages and substantial gardens, unlike the housing provided for the hundreds of employees of their works.

CHURCH STREET, COATBRIDGE.

This 1930s view of Church Street shows the changes that had taken place in only 35 years. The Horse Shoe Bar on the corner has become Gordon's the Tailor and on the opposite corner the Commercial Bank building has been built. Just up from the bank is the old Post Office, now demolished.

Gartsherrie Academy, Coatbridge

As well as providing churches, the Bairds also built numerous schools for their workers. The first of these, Gartsherrie Academy, was built in 1845. Designed to dominate the skyline along with Gartsherrie Church, the Academy originally housed four separate schools and has been further extended with an upper level. It now stands derelict with its windows boarded up and with a question mark hanging over its future.

Academy Street, Coatbridge

Academy Street still retains some of its stone villas but the bottom of the street has been altered numerous times. The steep streets in this part of town were a test for horses and carts and many a delivery-man would take a longer, circuitous route rather than attempt the hill on Church Street. The horse and cart in this view are parked across the road to stop the cart running away down the hill.

It would have been somewhere in this area that the bridge that originally gave Coatbridge its name was located. The bridge carried the main Glasgow to Airdrie road over the Gartsherrie Burn. The Coat part of the name is probably a corruption of Colt (the main landowners in the area). The cross was an important junction of almost every form of transport. When the canal was built it was carried over the Gartsherrie Burn by an aqueduct and a new bridge was built over the canal.

Until 1872 the railways went through the cross by means of a level crossing. The Whitelaw Fountain was erected in 1875 by grateful locals in recognition of the efforts made by Alexander Whitelaw to have a bridge built. The level crossing had become totally inadequate in a period of about forty years. With so much coal and ironstone going into the ironworks and finished products leaving, it had become dangerous. Whitelaw, a partner in Gartsherrie Ironworks, had the works railway re-aligned and an embankment and bridge built to replace the offending level crossing.

THE CROSS AND REGAL PICTURE HOUSE, COATBRIDGE.

A.6299.

The Whitelaw Fountain has been moved from its former spot beside the Royal Hotel because it too, like the level crossing, had become a traffic hazard. It now stands a few metres away from the middle of the busy roundabout on the South Circular Road. In the background is the Regal, once a majestic picture house and now Coatbridge's bingo hall. It was built in 1936.

24

Coatbridge's technical school has the distinction of being one of the world's first schools devoted to the teaching of science and technology. It was certainly Britain's first technical college. Like many of the town's public buildings, it was donated by the Bairds of Gartsherrie. It was built in 1890 when Coatbridge was still at the forefront of heavy industry but later became an annexe for the High School. In more recent times, with falling school rolls, the college is, like Gartsherrie Academy, surplus to requirements and boarded up.

High School, Coatbridge.

Behind the Technical School was Coatbridge High School. This imposing building met the kind of fate that seems to befall schools today and caught fire in 1929. The school was burned to the ground (no doubt to the great pleasure of its pupils) and demolished. A new extended school was built on the site and all that remains of the old school is the janitor's house on Muiryhall Street.

COATS PARISH CHURCH AND NEW SCHOOL, COATBRIDGE.

214575. J.V.

Dominating the skyline for miles around, Coats Parish Church is built on the highest spot in Coatbridge. It was built using money left by George Baird and opened in 1875. This early 1930s view predates the council housing that was later built in Muiryhall Street.

Coatbridge, with its rich mineral wealth and its vast trade in iron, was a mecca for railway promoters during the 19th Century. The first railway to reach the town was in 1826, although there had been some waggonways from the collieries to the Monkland Canal before that period. By the 1840s railways criss-crossed the Monklands and few parts of Coatbridge were further than a quarter of a mile from a railway line. These railways helped to shape the present day layout of the town. They separated Langloan, Dundyvan and Whifflet from Blairhill, Clifton and Sunnyside and their sidings took up vast amounts of space next to the ironworks and collieries. They even used up some of the ironworks waste as embankments and ballast for the tracks. In the 1880s the Caledonian Railway reached Coatbridge via their Glasgow to Airdrie line. The station building itself is long gone and has been replaced by bus shelters.

CROSS, LOOKING UP SUNNYSIDE ROAD, COATBRIDGE.

B.6072.

The first railway to reach Coatbridge was the Monkland & Kirkintilloch Railway in 1826. It was built to take coal and iron from Coatbridge and Airdrie to the Forth & Clyde Canal at Kirkintilloch. Once there, goods were trans-shipped to Bowling or Glasgow for export to England and the colonies. The M & K was one of the first railways in Scotland to use steam locomotives although horse power was predominant until 1831. Its network reached as far as Bo'ness and joined up with many of the important mineral lines in north Lanarkshire. Behind the Whitelaw Fountain is the LNER passenger station on one of the M & K's main lines. Also visible, top right, is one of the furnaces of Gartsherrie.

Sunnyside Road, Coatbridge

Looking across the Caledonian Railway Station, you could see the main station of their arch rivals, the North British Railway. With two competing railway companies each willing to build lines, there was much unnecessary duplication of services in and around Coatbridge. The sheer volume of freight traffic, however, more than made up for any losses in passenger revenue. Coatbridge Central closed to passengers in September 1930. The old Caledonian Railway line was electrified as part of the modernisation of the suburban lines around Glasgow.

Sunnyside Rd, Coatbridge.

Like the station, most of the buildings in Sunnyside Road have gone. Piecemeal re-development has taken place along Sunnyside Road. At its junction with Main Street, Sunnyside Road has fared well but further up, towards Gartsherrie and Sunnyside Station, little remains of this once bustling thoroughfare.

COATBRIDGE, CHURCH STREET
FROM SUNNYSIDE STATION.

Church Street has suffered the same fate as much of Sunnyside Road. All of the shops have been demolished and all that remains are the bungalows at the top of the street.

The first trams in public service in Coatbridge ran on the 8th of February 1904. There were proposals in 1871 for a horse drawn tramway from Airdrie which would join with the Glasgow Tramways at Duke Street, Glasgow. A rival scheme was promoted but both ideas were abandoned shortly after. Over twenty years were to pass before the next proposals. Between 1896 and 1900 there were numerous proposed tramways for the Monklands. The new Tramway Acts made it much easier to promote and build tramways and there were competing consortiums all wanting to build their own lines. Eventually the Airdrie & Coatbridge Tramways Company won the battle to transport the workforce to and from the mines and ironworks. Almost 9,500 people were carried on the tramways' four operational cars on that first Monday. By the Thursday, upwards of 27,000 people had travelled on the new trams.

It is difficult to imagine trams running down Main Street today. Taken from the fountain, this view shows, on the left, the Royal Hotel which was demolished to make way for the Airdrie Savings Bank in 1920. This part of the Main Street has suffered badly from the re-developers who, in the 1970s and early 1980s, managed to totally destroy the character of the street. On the right, there is now a concrete and brick shopping complex and the street has been narrowed to restrict vehicle access.

A photographer was still enough of a novelty in 1905 or 1906 to attract this amount of interest. This part of Main Street has now been pedestrianised. The tram has just passed St. Patrick's Church on its way to the terminus at Langloan. St. Patrick's was built in 1896 on land donated by the Bairds and was built to serve the large Irish Catholic population as well as many of the Highlanders who had left their crofts. Coatbridge's population had been swelled by the influx of people all willing to work in the wretched and dangerous conditions of the many works and mines.

MAIN STREET, COATBRIDGE

Main Street decorated for the 1937 Coronation. Coia's Central Cafe and the Airdrie Savings Bank are prominent on the right. In this area and up Sunnyside Street, at the turn of this century, there were almost twenty pubs and inns. Drunkenness was a problem even in 1793 when there were thirty pubs in Old Monkland serving a population of only about 4000. The Parish Minister, writing about the habits of the locals, was concerned about the "pernicious effects to the health and morals of the people". Nowadays, the favourite tipple of the Monklands is Buckfast Fortified Wine (brewed by the monks of Buckfast Abbey to a centuries old recipe) or so *The Herald* would have you believe!

MAIN STREET, COATBRIDGE.

A6290

Looking the other way, towards the town centre, this view dates from some thirty years later. By the 1930s, buses were beginning to cut into tram revenues as they were faster and more convenient. Enormous changes have taken place since and, sadly, like the ironworks, the Theatre Royal is but a distant memory. This part of the Main Street has been totally obliterated and is looked down on by the Jackson Street flats.

Theatre, Main Street, Coatbridge

The 2000 seat Theatre Royal looked out over the Phoenix and Clifton Iron Works. This was the iron heart of the town, where iron works jostled with shops and houses for space alongside the main street and the Monkland Canal. Coming out of the theatre after a show, the noise, light and smell of the Clifton Ironworks must have surpassed any show inside.

This is an early 1920s view of Main Street looking towards the Clifton Iron Works. Lorries were beginning to take over from horses and carts for local deliveries. Many of the trucks were ex-army surplus. Creature comforts for the lorry driver were poor. His vehicle had solid rubber tyres, little or no suspension, hand starting, no weather protection and was limited to a top speed of about 20 mph.

LOVELY COATBRIDGE.   Robb's Series.

The main reason that Coatbridge took such a long period to adopt Burgh status was that when it did, it would have to comply with many of the mid 19th Century Health and Pollution Acts. By staying a conglomeration of small villages, the town was exempt from these acts and the ironmasters could boost their profits by spending less on measures to limit the pollution. By 1885, however, there was an increasing call for the Town to become a Burgh. A special Act of Parliament was passed so that the town could become exempt from some of the legislation. As a result, the town was probably the most polluted in Britain even up to the 1920s.

"SOMEWHERE THE SUN IS SHINING"
BUT NOT IN
COATBRIDGE.

Even at the turn of this century when these two postcards were issued, the town had a reputation for smoke, dust and noise. By that time, there were no open topped blast furnaces, but still during the day, the smoke was unbearable and at night the sky was lit up for miles around by the light of the blast furnaces. When these were open-topped it was possible to read a paper by their yellow glow even in the middle of the night. On a foggy day, everyone would wear scarves around their faces to keep out the lethal smog.

The Calder Iron Works were the first in the local area and were established about 1795 by a consortium of Glasgow Weavers. The works went bust and were sold to a partnership of William Dixon, James Creelman and David Mushet. After two years the partnership was dissolved and William Dixon became the sole owner. Dixon was born in Northumberland and had moved to Glasgow to make his fortune. He succeeded and purchased the iron works as well as the estates of Faskine and Palacecraig. He died in 1824 and his works were left to two of his sons. William bought out John, his elder brother and extended the works. The Calder Iron works were built in the valley of the Calder Water so that the furnaces could easily be fed from the top. They produced their last ingots of iron in 1921. This locomotive, Calder No1, was built in 1861 and was finally scrapped in 1927. It would have been used within the works for shifting waggons and was one of a fleet of around eighteen locomotives.

Founded in 1830, the Gartsherrie Ironworks were the largest in Coatbridge. Owned by the Bairds, they were expanded to a maximum of sixteen blast furnaces. The Bairds were local farmers who had made a small fortune in coal mining, opening their first colliery at Rochsolloch sometime about 1816. This fortune they ploughed into the iron works as well as into extensive reserves of ironstone and coal. By 1868, they owned four ironworks in Ayrshire as well as numerous coal and ironstone mines. By the 1880s, the profits from iron manufacture were not enough and Bairds were the first to diversify into bi-products. From around 1850 waste gases from the blast furnaces were used to heat the blast but by the 1880s this was not enough. Increasing costs of imported raw materials led to the building of a recovery plant for coal tar and ammonia in 1880. By the 1930s Gartsherrie had a cement plant and coking ovens as well. These chemical works, which became a feature of most of the ironworks, did nothing to help the already foul air in Coatbridge.

The Bairds also owned their own small railway network. It served the Gartsherrie works as well as transporting coal and iron ore from the various collieries to the ironworks. The locos were also used to transport slag and waste from the ironworks to the many slagheaps and bings close at hand. Locomotive No.1 was built in 1874 and lasted until 1938 before being scrapped. It was built in Dubs' works in Glasgow's south side. The driver is almost certainly David Forsyth who was still the driver in 1934. Gartsherrie Works are now no more, having lasted until 1967. The Freight Liner terminal has been built on the site. Gartsherrie House, latterly home of the Bairds, suffered the same fate.

Summerlee Iron Works, Coatbridge.

Erected by Wilson & Co. in 1836, Summerlee was the largest works after Gartsherrie. It was situated on the Gartsherrie, Hornock & Summerlee branch of the Monkland Canal. Originally, there was a sulphur works located here, but the branch canal was built to serve two coal mines owned by the Bairds. When Gartsherrie and Summerlee opened, the branch canal was completed. When it opened, Summerlee had only a couple of furnaces in blast but at its peak it had eight in operation. Like Gartsherrie, Summerlee was the only other blast furnace to close down on Sundays. All of the others were in blast seven days per week, much to the annoyance of the local ministers.

Captured for posterity below one of the 50 feet high blast furnaces of Summerlee are some of the men responsible for making the fortunes of the Wilsons. This hardy lot would have been responsible for charging the furnace with coal and ironstone as well as tapping the furnace for smelted pig iron. It was called pig iron because, when the furnace was tapped, the iron was let into a row of troughs that looked like suckling piglets. Theirs was a dirty, dangerous and thirsty job. Their mates would have been kept busy supplying them with beer to quash their thirsts. Sixty hour weeks in the high temperatures and arid atmosphere of the blast furnace would have been rewarded with about £1 per week in the 1880s. Fifty years later there was little demand for Summerlee iron and the blast furnaces in Summerlee were damped down for ever in 1930. Taking their place today is Scotland's noisiest museum.

Carnbroe Ironworks were founded in 1838 and had six blast furnaces. They were owned by Merry & Cunningham who proceeded to buy Glengarnock and Ardeer Ironworks in Ayrshire in 1843 and 1854 respectively. This locomotive, pictured at Carnbroe North signalbox, was purchased new in 1862 and was the eleventh locomotive that Barclay's of Kilmarnock produced. The ironworks closed in 1921. Their remains lie hidden under Carnbroe's sprawling housing estate.

Phœnix & Clifton Iron Works, Coatbridge.

As well as the blast furnaces providing raw pig iron, Coatbridge boasted many smaller concerns producing finished products such as castings, shovels, iron plate and tubes. These were spread along the banks of the canal and used it for transport as well as for cooling water. Sometimes the canal steamed away. At night this steam, the smoke and the dull glow from the puddling furnaces must have given this area an eerie, ghostly appearance and the battering of steam hammers and other machinery would have been enough to wake the residents of Old Monkland churchyard. The Clifton Iron Works closed in May 1913 and was followed in August 1921 by the Phoenix Iron Works.

Opened in 1858, Rochsolloch Iron Works were capable of producing 200 tons of finished malleable iron per month by 1868. The works had twenty six puddling and two heating furnaces in 1901. Producing malleable iron was very labour intensive as there wasn't a mechanical method that could simulate a puddling furnace. Pig iron was brittle and of little use to anyone making tools or iron bar. In a puddling furnace a man would work the pig iron until it had lost its brittleness and was malleable. By the turn of this century, steel was becoming cheaper than malleable iron and in 1912 the Scottish Iron & Steel Company was formed by the amalgamation of thirteen ironworks. These included Rochsolloch, Phoenix, Clifton, Waverley, Drumpellier and the North British Works. This combine gradually began a process of converting some works to steel re-rolling and closing down others. In 1916 they began construction of their own steelworks at Northburn, next to the Waverley works. Opened in 1920, these were the first steelworks in Scotland to be electrically powered throughout.

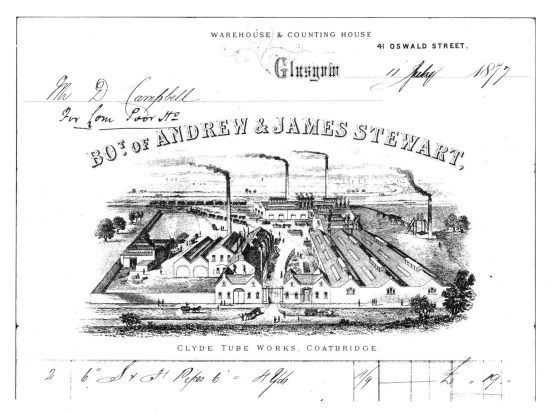

WAREHOUSE & COUNTING HOUSE

41 OSWALD STREET,

Glasgow ___11 July___ 1877

Mr D Campbell

For Com Poor Ho

BOT OF ANDREW & JAMES STEWART,

CLYDE TUBE WORKS, COATBRIDGE.

| 2 | 6" S & Ft Pipes 6' = 4 Yds | | 4/9 | | £ | " 19 " |

Coatbridge has been a centre for tube manufacture since the 1840s. After starting production in 1860 in Glasgow, Andrew Stewart moved to Coatbridge in 1867 and built Clyde Tube Works. After amalgamating with the Clydesdale Iron & Steel Company in 1890, they joined forces with their major competitor, James Menzies, in 1898 to become Scotland's largest tube manufacturer. In 1903 they merged with Lloyd and Lloyd of Birmingham to become Stewarts & Lloyds. By the time they bought the Scottish Tube Company in 1932, they were the largest producers of tubes in Britain. Much of their output was exported. In the early 1930s, Stewarts & Lloyds were responsible for a mass migration from Coatbridge to Corby. The effects of depression, closure of the iron works following a short-lived wartime boom and a collapse in mining led to an unemployment rate of about 40%. Stewarts & Lloyds were building a new, integrated steelworks at Corby and there was a promise of a new life, in good housing with a job. Hundreds left Coatbridge between 1930 and 1935 to live and work in Northamptonshire.

Muiryhall Street has, like many of the streets in Coatdyke, been ravaged by town planners and slum clearers. Little remains of old Coatdyke. Not only has the industry gone but most of the housing has also been demolished. All of the buildings on the left have gone to be replaced by one of the many gap sites that are to be found in Coatbridge today. All that remains is the fountain erected by Andrew Stewart in 1886 to commemorate Coatbridge attaining Burgh status. It seems a shame that these houses weren't upgraded and enlarged rather than demolished.

Main Street, Coatdyke. In late 1921, Glasgow Corporation took over the tramways and by May 1922 they had started work on the Baillieston-Coatbridge extension. This would connect the tramway into the huge Glasgow network. An extra track was laid along most of the route as well. The new regime took pride in their new network and the trams were faster and more frequent. By 1925 the new line was open and it was possible to travel from Ferguslie Mills, Paisley to Airdrie for 10d. Many of the services had been taken over by larger Glasgow trams and this tramcar, No.4, was scrapped in 1930. The last trams ran in November 1956, and most of the track removed soon after. The tram depot at Jackson Street is now a furniture store.

The small group of children captured for posterity are looking down from Rochsolloch Road on to Rochsolloch Iron-works. Nowadays the view is totally different. Rochsolloch Road has been extensively re-developed. These houses are gone and have been replaced by newer flats. The ironworks are no more and the view beyond the railway is now of Sikeside and Carnbroe housing estates.

It is difficult to imagine this scene today. Apart from the school at the top of the hill, nothing remains of Kippen Street. This view is from Rochsolloch Road. Wholesale demolition took place after the Second World War and new houses were built. The last thirty years have seen Coatbridge expand. The urban sprawl has swallowed up greenfield sites as well as areas of older housing like this. Overcrowding has been almost eradicated.

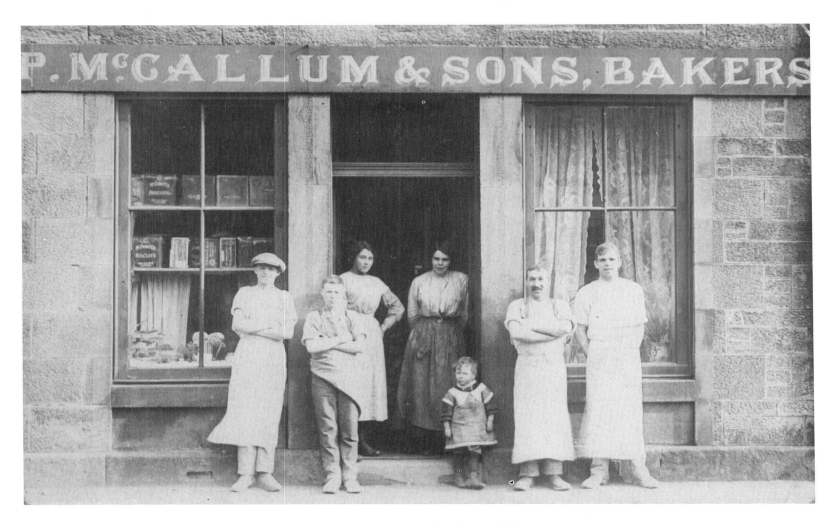

154 KippenStreet, Coatdyke about 1910.

Burgh of Coatbridge Police Force November 1911.

Back row: Constables Chalmers Dawson Clark Sanderson Fairservice J. McDonald Bruce
Third row: Constables Scott Henderson Cowie Jackson Weir Innes Blair Court Smyth Gilchrist
Second row: Constables Turner Brown Broadfoot Lockhart Thompson Kane Hector Morrison Mathieson Pirie McMullan Garrow McPherson Orr
First row: Constables Robertson Meston Acting Sgt. Forrest Sgts. Gordon Barclay Wm. Ewan W.Mcdonald George Scott Sgts. Irvine Borthwick Constables Cooper Bell Wm. McDonald
(Inspector)(Chief Const.)(Inspector)

56